EYAM PLAGUE

1665 - 1666

by

John Clifford

First Published in 1989
Revised in 1993 and 1995
Revised and enlarged in 2003

John Clifford
Eyam
Derbyshire

ISBN 0-9544666-0-8

CONTENTS

		page
Chapter 1	The General Scene	1
Chapter 2	The Local Scene	5
Chapter 3	The Plague Arrives in Eyam	7
Chapter 4	The Time of Decision	13
Chapter 5	Climax...	20
Chapter 6	...and Decline	24
Chapter 7	The Human Dimension	26
Chapter 8	The Last Word	35
Bibliography		41

PHOTOGRAPHS

Opposite page 8   *Eyam village*
The Tailor's Cottage

Opposite page 9   *Plague Cottages, Eyam*
The Church of St. Lawrence, Eyam

Opposite page 28   *The Riley Graves (the graves of the Hancock family) beyond Riley Wood*

Catherine Mompesson's Tomb on Plague Sunday

Opposite page 29   *The Boundary Stone*
Mompesson's Well

This book is dedicated to my wife, Francine, who realised that if she could not alter my obsession with the wonderful story of this village she must join it.

She spent countless hours tracing the life histories of those gallant survivors of the tragedy.

It is also dedicated to the late Alan Goodfellow, M.A. who, sixty years ago, sowed the seeds of my great love of history.

PREFACE

Many people have written the story of Eyam Plague since it was first set down by Mompesson himself. His own son George gave his version of what happened, to Dr Richard Meade, who published '*A Discourse on Plague*' in 1721. This account, in the light of new evidence, seems to be much nearer the truth than has been believed for many years, but since George was only four years old in 1665, and was not in Eyam for the whole of the plague period, it was thought that his memory may have been at fault, and he was considered an unreliable witness.

Anna Seward, the Swan of Lichfield, the daughter of an eighteenth century rector of Eyam, wrote about the subject in 1774, and John Howard, the penal reformer, a friend of the Sewards, who was deeply interested in the study of contagious diseases, researched in the village which he visited on occasions when preparing his book about the principal Lazarettos in Europe (1789).

William Wood, the Victorian Historian, who lived in the village published '*The History and the Antiquities of Eyam*', which ran into many editions spanning the greater part of the nineteenth century and reached a wider public. The book is noteworthy because he included a detailed account of the plague based on the oral tradition, but he tended to be carried away by Victorian romanticism, and is not always accurate. For example, his estimate of the size of the population of the village, which was challenged in 1881, some fifteen years after Wood had died, by the Rev'd John Green, William Wood's own rector, and also by no less a person than the Secretary of the Census Office in that year. It was eventually doubted by Wood's own publishers in the 1895 edition.

In more recent times, the late Clarence Daniel, another Eyam man whose family roots are traceable back to pre-plague days, carried out further detailed research, which he published under the title of '*The Story of Eyam Plague*' and which includes a guide to the village. He also spent much of his life collecting material, which formed the basis of the collection in his private museum, which now is incorporated in the Eyam Museum collection, where the story of Eyam Plague and the post plague redevelopment of the village are graphically told. Most particularly, he kept alive the interest in the story.

Some of the differences between these early accounts are quite significant and will be examined closely. Other sources from which the present booklet is compiled, and which should be read by the serious scholar, include among contemporary source material the first volume of the Parish Register, which combines the Bishop's Transcripts, and which is published by the Derbyshire Record Society, and the numerous wills and inventories, which are to be located in the Staffordshire Joint Records Office in Lichfield. These have disclosed family relationships that have long been forgotten, and shed light on the social position and occupations of many of the victims.

There is a growing list of works on the subject of plague in general and of the outbreak in Eyam in particular, in both fact and fiction, which will be found in the bibliography.

Finally I must express my gratitude to the Rev. D. G. Shaw, Rector of Eyam for his advice, wise counsel and support, and to Dr O'Sullivan, Director of the Derbyshire Record Office in Matlock, and to the late Mrs Jane Hampartumian at the Lichfield Joint Record Office for permission to reproduce some of their material.

Chapter 1

The General Scene

Since this book first appeared fourteen years ago, when bubonic plague was, in the western world at least, confined to the pages of history, a lot has happened that has brought it forward in a new, but equally sinister light. Much new material has been published in book form or presented on the stage and small screen over the last twenty years, both fact and fiction, which has generated wide public interest, not only on the subject of the disease in itself but especially on its impact on the village of Eyam.

Primarily bubonic plague is a rat disease and in general terms does not normally affect human beings until the rat population is reduced to a point where there are insufficient rats to sustain it. Whilst the disease is found in several rodent species, it is most commonly found in what we usually term the black rat, though this is not an accurate description and it should properly be called the house rat or ship rat, which indicates its preferred habitat. In this country it is now rare, and is found almost exclusively and in limited numbers in port and dockland areas. The rat with which we are familiar, the commonly called brown rat, (which again is a misnomer, for colour is an unreliable guide to either species) prefers a less domesticated habitat. Though frequently to be found only a matter of a few metres from us, and often in large numbers, it prefers our drains and sewers and so lives beneath our feet. As a plague transmitter it is less of a problem, but no less of a worldwide menace. Neither rat is indigenous to these shores but both have been with us a long time. It is generally thought that the house rat (*Rattus rattus*), appeared in Britain somewhere between the Norman Conquest and the fourteenth century, though this has been challenged recently and there are those who would put its appearance earlier. The brown rat (*Rattus norvegicus*), which is the more dominant species, did not reach England until 1729, so it had not appeared at the time of the plague in the 17th century. It was certainly not around at the time of the Great Pestilence, the so called Black Death in the middle of the 14th century.

The rat is host to a flea, which itself is the carrier of the plague bacilli. The fleas feed on the blood of their host, and when an infected flea feeds, it leaves bacilli in the rat's body, which bring about a rapid death. If a healthy flea bites an infected rat the bacilli are taken in during its meal. These bacilli block the flea's food tract so that its hunger is not assuaged. It therefore seeks more food, frequently from another rat, and by regurgitating its undigested previous meal, which still contains bacilli, continues the cycle, i.e. flea-to-rat-to-flea-to-rat. In the absence of sufficient rats, an infected flea will take human blood, or rarely, blood from other small mammals, but there is no flea-to-man-to-flea infection. That is to say that an infected person will not infect a healthy flea. The fleas must gain a 'top-up' of infection from a rodent.

The usual course of bubonic plague in humans is a massive infection centred on the lymph nodes, and principally those that are in the groin area (bubo is the Greek word for groin). However the lungs can also become infected, giving rise to pneumonic plague, which is less common but much more dangerous, since once established, it can be spread by direct human contact, without the assistance of the rodents. The patient will sneeze and cough sputum, often mixed with infected blood and spread by the droplets in the expulsion. This is a very simplified description of how the disease is spread and there are, of course, other complications and many other symptoms. The 17th century doctors reckoned that there were 33 as displayed in Eyam Museum. When their lists are compared with a modern diagnosis it is clear that they knew what they were looking at.

The disease is more dangerous in the warmer weather, and in England people were correct when they thought that the winter months would bring relief from it, though they were working from false premises, even though they reached a generally correct solution. It was always much more common in warmer countries, and is still a danger in Asia and parts of Africa and in America, though to only a very limited area in the U.S.A where it is not an urban problem. A warm climate, poor sanitation, poverty, filth and squalor are all part of the habitat of both commensal and sylvatic rats.

The roots of mediaeval disease were once thought to lie in astrology, and 'scientific' explanations of the cause of sickness were sought in a study of the heavens. In particular they were considered to have been brought about by the conjunction of the planets. For instance, in Johannes Nohl '*The Black Death*' writes that in March 1345 there was a conjunction of Saturn, Mars and Jupiter in the House of Aquarius, which was felt at that time to mean the onset of an epidemic on a cataclysmic scale. The Black Death erupted in 1347.

There was a deep religious belief that the arrival of plague was punishment for sin and as will be noted later this view was held in Eyam. Many believed that the only antidote was to seek Divine forgiveness through prayer and repentance, and that to active take steps to cure themselves would certainly serve only to make their position and their sin worse in the eyes of God. For those of a less deeply inclined religious view, the way was to purge oneself firstly, of all possible sin by indulging in totally riotous and wicked living and debauchery and in a final act of commitment seek total forgiveness. Such a course may have held certain attractions for some.

Devoted people, both in the medical profession and among the clergy gave dedicated service to the sick in the face of all the odds and many gave their own lives in consequence, but they were fighting against great ignorance and greater fear.

A study of the scene in London shows how the civic authorities fought in a losing and seemingly ever worsening situation to maintain control, and they acted within the scope of their knowledge and their legal powers to contain the outbreaks of plague when they occurred. Orders were published to limit the movement of people, both in and out of London, but they could not be enforced and were seldom effective. Theatres and other places of entertainment where people could meet in large numbers were closed to contain mass movements. People were confined to their homes when a case of plague was discovered, and the resulting suffering for the healthy among the sick was very harsh. The total number of deaths from plague in London in 1665-6 is estimated at between 70,000 and 100,000, and even these figures may be too low because of the devious tricks that people used to try to disguise the true cause of death in order to avoid immuration.

Medical treatment was primitive in the extreme as will be seen. The modern sulphonamides in use in our own times, which were unknown, even in the first quarter of the 20th century, have certainly proved more effective than the herb remedies, the nostrums and charms on which they relied in Stuart times, and the old herbals make interesting but curious reading. Most people trusted in the doubtful efficacy of the herbs that grew around them, but many unsuspecting folk were duped by rogues and charlatans and wore charms or cabbalistic signs sold to them at high prices. Some women put their trust in sweet smelling flowers, which would freshen the malodorous air, or carried pomanders stuffed with herbs and spices, whilst their men folk preferred to smoke a pipe of tobacco. In London, as Samuel Pepys tells us, they attempted to clear the air by burning coal in braziers placed at intervals in the principal streets.

Reliance was often placed on poultices, which would draw the lump or bubo, which gives the disease its name, to a head, in the hope that when it burst the infection could be drawn off. One contemporary 'cure' asserted that the drawing or 'ripening' process could be speeded up if a live chicken or pigeon, or in cases of extreme need, a toad, were to be strapped to the patient's body, so that the creature's vent was placed directly over the bubo. The constant warm temperature of the bird's body would no doubt induce the bubo to swell and erupt much more quickly. The theory then being, that if the creature had been positioned correctly, the poison coming from the burst bubo would be drawn in to its own body by a kind of siphoning action, so that it would die. The process was to be repeated until the bird was no longer affected or harmed in any way, which meant that the cure had been effective and the patient would recover.

This seems fanciful in the extreme until one reads that during the course of scientific research undertaken by the Americans during the Vietnam War, traces of aureomycin, one of the drugs that is now used as a cure, were found to be occurring naturally in the soil. This suggests that poultry in that country in the course of their natural habit of gritting could be taking the drug into their digestive systems, and so by the natural processes of ingestion, digestion and defecation, it is possible that by using this 'cure', traces of the drug could have been deposited on the erupting bubo. When we then add to this the knowledge that bubonic plague spread from the Far East, it is arguably possible that as the disease spread westwards, some knowledge of a primitive treatment may have followed in its wake.

Some remedies were of the foulest kind and there seemed a general belief that the more repugnant they were the more they were likely to cure. Robert Wilkinson in his '*Fireside Book of Deadly Diseases*' summarises the treatments advocated by contemporary physicians, and Johannes Nohl examines these cures in great detail. Both animal and human body wastes were incorporated with other fluids to make a medicinal drink, and one is left wondering whether the remedy was worse than the disease, and it certainly frequently led to the same end. On a marginally lighter note one may consider the belief that raising the body temperature was harmful and exercise or strenuous activities would endanger one. On these grounds it was suggested that taking a hot bath should at all costs be avoided. One doctor ordered a large mastiff to be laid on his patient's chest for several hours. He added that "she was a big woman and could stand it", whilst others swore by garlic or onions in unsociable quantities.

Chapter 2

The Local Scene

Tucked away behind the hills that form Middleton Dale about twelve miles along the road from Chesterfield to Manchester via Chapel-en-le-Frith lies the village of Eyam. Even today one can easily miss the finger post pointing to the right up the steep and wooded valley of Eyam Dale, about half a mile out of the village of Stoney Middleton, on the A623.

Three hundred years ago it was a truly remote and isolated spot. The roads used by today's visitors had not been built and the approaches to the village were by the rough, narrow tracks that are still taken to view some of the ancient memorials of the plague days. The nearest towns - Matlock, Chesterfield and Buxton - and the city of Sheffield, all lie about twelve or thirteen miles away, and Bakewell, the local market town, is seven miles to the south. Eyam is one of a cluster of ancient villages lying on the slopes above the valley of the River Derwent after it has wound its way through the beautiful Hope Valley which takes its name from the village of Hope which lies nearer the head of the valley.

There were settlements hereabouts at least as far back as the early part of the Bronze Age, and the area was important to the Romans. Near the village of Brough, about five miles north-west of Eyam, was the Roman fort of Navio, which protected their lines of communication to Buxton (Aquae Armentiae), and also their interests in the lead mining industry, which for many centuries was of prime importance in the valley. A few Roman artefacts have been found in Eyam, but it was not a settlement.

Eyam as a village was established in Anglo-Saxon times and a magnificent Anglian stone cross, dating from the late eighth century now stands in the church yard. It was not always there, for it was a preaching cross serving as a centre of worship for the group of local hamlets long before the church was built. The name Eyam or Aiune, which is one of the earliest spellings of the name, is Saxon, and means a settlement by the water, for it is the presence of water in abundance that is one of the reasons for the establishment of the village, which nestles on the slopes of a massive shale and gritstone hill to the north, which forces the river into a huge curve.

Much of Eyam's prosperity came from the many lead mines, the remains of which are found in the vicinity, and in the eighteenth century, the rector had one of the most lucrative livings in the country, derived largely from the lead tithes. That industry is no more, and it was partly the abundant water supply that destroyed it, for, as the mines were sunk deeper, the problems of taking away the surplus water proved too costly, and too difficult.

Eyam is still a working village, and though it attracts huge numbers of tourists each year, it is neither a picture postcard scene, nor a museum. It lies within the Peak National Park, and both the Peak District National Park Authority and the villagers themselves are determined that its character shall not be destroyed. The tourist interest lies chiefly in a story of heroism and dedication that is over 300 years old, which is constantly told, but is never stale, and though modern theories may come and go, the villagers hold to the traditional tale, and tell it with pride. It is that story which will now unfold.

In the 300 years or so from 1347, there were frequent outbreaks of bubonic plague in all the towns and countless villages throughout the land. Many smaller settlements disappeared from the map altogether, and of some village sites, not even a name survives. Everybody has heard of the Plague of London in 1665, which was followed by the Great Fire in the following year. That date, like 1066, is one of the landmarks of British history, known to every school child and remembered by its parents, but there were many other plagues in London, and some killed a greater percentage of the population than the one that is generally remembered.

Similarly, there were several other outbreaks of plague up and down the country in 1665, most of which have been forgotten. The outbreak that occurred in Eyam is the one great exception.

The origin of the outbreak has been challenged many times recently, and the controversy will continue, but the traditional tale is deeply rooted, and will stand the test of time.

Immediately to the west of the church yard is a cluster of cottages, dating from at least the 17th. century, and long known as the Plague Cottages. Three of these stand beside the road, and it is in the middle of these three that the story starts.

Chapter 3

The Plague Arrives in Eyam

William Wood tells us that in 1665, there was living in this cottage with her two young sons, a woman whom the oral tradition names as Mary Cooper, the widow of a lead miner. That summer, which is recorded as being long and hot, had attracted many visitors, particularly at the time of the Village Wakes towards the end of August, and she had taken in a lodger called George Viccars, who was a travelling tailor. Wood does not record exactly when he arrived, or if he was a regular visitor, calling on Eyam, as part of an established round, or whether he was a stranger, hoping to profit from the temporary prosperity that the visitors would bring.

In the account given by George Mompesson, the son of the rector, Viccars is referred to as a servant, and for a long time it has been suggested that the memory of a four year old was at fault, for there seemed no likelihood of a widow of a lead miner, being in a position to have servants. However we now know by reference to his will that when Edward Cooper, who described himself as a yeoman, died in 1664, he was literate and a relatively prosperous man, leaving effects recorded in his inventory, worth over £90, and which included a Bible and other books; that he had recently purchased some land from John Wilson and was owed over £40 in outstanding debts; and that he was a friend of Thomas Wright of Unthank near Holmesfield, which lies a few miles away near Sheffield. Indeed, in naming Thomas Wright as his executor he describes him as his "beloved and trusty friend", which is not the sort of language that a poor miner would use of such an important person. The Wright family also had an estate in Great Longstone to the west of Eyam and still are the principal family in Eyam, living in the hall which was built, by the same Thomas Wright a few years after the plague. The Coopers were therefore obviously not scraping a living.

It is now certain that in March 1665 about five months before the plague broke out, Mary Cooper had remarried, her new husband being Alexander Hadfield, whose own will states very clearly that he was a tailor. This second marriage is underlined by Mary's father, Thomas Mosley, who refers to her as Mary Hadfield in his will, in which he leaves her merely the traditional shilling, presumably because she had little need of a legacy from him, for by then she was still wealthy, Alexander having died of the plague, and leaving an inventory of goods valued at over £60.

In 1721 Dr. Richard Meade in his book '*A Discourse on Plague*' quoting George Mompesson, the son of the Rector over the plague period wrote that "a box of materials relating to his trade" was delivered to the village tailor, and that "a servant who opened the aforesaid box, finding they were damp was ordered to dry them by the fire". The tailor would be very likely to have an assistant, (which in the eyes of a five year old, as George Mompesson was at the time of the plague, could well be described as a servant). A skilled workman at that period was called a journeyman, which means a man working for a daily wage (i.e. from the French journée), which may eventually have given rise to confusion, and in the eyes of later generations have come to mean a travelling man. However it needs only a little imagination to believe that Hadfield himself was the travelling tailor and was perhaps away from home when the materials arrived. This would explain why he did not die until almost twelve months later and then among the Hadfield family, suggesting that if he had been away when the plague broke, he had not returned to his wife but had sought the safety of the members of his family at that time unaffected by the infection.

Tradition has it that the box came from London, arriving about the end of August or very early in September, and contained cloth, which another legend says was made by the weavers of Canterbury. Another plausible theory is that in order to introduce more recent fashions to his customers, the tailor had bought second hand clothing. This may have been discarded by wealthy London residents, who were seeking the very latest fashion trends to be seen at the royal court, or perhaps removed from one, who unknown to him had actually died of plague. These 'nearly new' styles he would use as patterns for his own customers.

Traditionally the contents of the box were found on arrival to be damp, and were therefore laid out to dry off. Viccars, we are told, became ill shortly after opening the box. The modern interpretation is that the cloth harboured rat fleas or their eggs, which were infected with the bacilli which caused bubonic plague, and that when they were released as the cloth was unfolded and shaken, they moved out in search of nourishment. Though they normally fed on the blood of the rat they would also take food from other sources, and so it was that Viccars was infected. Whilst he would have been aware that he had been bitten, neither he, nor anyone near him would have made the connection between the flea bites and his death a some days later.

The disease strikes quickly, and within about five or six days of the appearance of the first symptoms, Viccars was dead. This probably occurred on the 6th of September, for his funeral took place on the 7th. His grave is not known but it is very unlikely that a workman who was not a native of the

Eyam village

The Tailor's Cottage

Plague Cottages, Eyam

The Church of St. Lawrence, Eyam

village, and without a family around, would ever have had a headstone. Nobody in the village would go to the expense of providing one, and had he died from any other cause he would probably have been forgotten about by Christmas, and certainly would have left no other record to posterity than an entry in the parish register of an obscure Derbyshire village. Following a conversation a few years ago, with a visitor to the village, it is now thought that Viccars was married but living away from home and that he was survived by his children, whose present day descendants are aware of their family history.

The disease, having claimed its first victim, takes about a fortnight to establish itself in a community and so we find that on September 22nd young Edward Cooper was buried. On the 23rd, the burial of Peter Hawksworth who lived close by was recorded. On the 26th, Thomas Thorpe, another near neighbour was buried, to be followed on the 30th by his daughter, Mary, who was twelve years old. On the same day, Sarah Syddall, whose family lived on the opposite side of the road was another victim. With six deaths in the space of three weeks, in four neighbouring houses, there was obviously something very seriously wrong, and it takes little imagination to sense the fear and panic that would be felt by others living close by, and indeed, by the whole village. Today, in an age in which there is vast medical knowledge there is still something of a mild hysteria when we are confronted with sudden outbreaks of disease, as in India in 1994, when plague broke out near Surat, a story that was taken up by the media and enlarged out of all proportion with a consequent spread of alarm. How much greater must have been their fear in 1665 on the arrival of an incurable killer.

The nature of the disease has been challenged in recent times, and there are those like Graham Twigg and Brian Robinson who have suggested typhus, anthrax or measles as the more likely cause of death in Eyam. Anna Seward, the daughter of the village rector at the time of the plague centenary may have unwittingly added weight to the anthrax theory. She wrote that in 1757 five workmen digging on the hillside above the village uncovered some rotting linen material. "In consequence they all succumbed to a putrid fever and three of them died to be quickly followed by several others in the village".

In fact however there were only ten deaths recorded in Eyam in the whole of that year, spread at fairly regular intervals throughout the whole twelve months, though there was however a much heavier mortality late in 1759, for which no explanation has been offered. In suggesting the resilience of the bacillus over a period of about ninety years Miss Seward may have added weight to the anthrax theory, but the numerous wills and inventories of the plague victims which list large numbers of surviving livestock, make it seem improbable. More recently Susan Scott and Christopher Duncan have offered haemorrhagic plague as the only possible source of such a disaster.

There is some similarity with plague in the initial stages of typhus but the strong arguments voiced in favour of this theory imply that the people of the day were less precise in their diagnosis, which is to some extent true, though, as noted earlier, there were some thirty three symptoms of plague for which they would be looking, which suggests a more sophisticated approach. Paul Slack, a Fellow of Exeter College, Oxford, states in his book, '*The Impact of Plague in Tudor & Stuart England*' that "by the middle of the 17th century the word plague increasingly referred to a special and usually identifiable disease." Whereas typhus had been rife in the armies of the Civil War, where there were grossly insanitary conditions, problems of this nature would be unlikely to exist in a small rural area even though it would be less hygienic than today.

With no scientific background upon which to draw, the onset of the disease would only be explained in religious or supernatural terms. It was thought by some to be the wrath of God, visited upon a sinful people, who could only be propitiated by prayer and repentance, or by submission, for if it was a Divine punishment, it had to be endured at all costs. Many devout people refused what preventive measures were available lest they should they should further anger the Almighty. The more superstitious of the people searched their memories for signs and portents of their impending doom as carefully as others pondered on their sins, and they were of course not hard to find.

It was recalled in Eyam that earlier in the year some village lads had allowed some cows to enter the church, and they had fouled the nave, and this they felt was surely enough to invoke God's wrath. Others remembered that they had heard the sounds of Gabriel Hounds (the spirits of unbaptised children) as they hovered in the air over the moor above the village, and white crickets had been seen on domestic hearths, both of which they were quite certain were clear indications of doom!

With no effective remedies the natural inclination for most people was for flight, (this was of course not possible for those with the fundamentalist belief that punishment had to be endured), whilst the only effective form of control was quarantine. There is no record of how many people left the village in those early weeks and months and it may be more than is popularly supposed for as will be shown later William Wood's estimate of the size of the village population has been seriously challenged.

On the other hand whilst the more affluent landowning families like the

Sheldons were known to have left, it was impossible for the poorer landlords, the smaller mine owners, tenant farmers and labourers to abandon their livelihoods. There was no way that they could lock up and leave. For those who did escape, there were other factors apart from the purely financial, to be considered; they must have had somewhere else to go and have access to another house away from the plague area, or friends or relatives who would take them in, and the means of getting there. Such a journey would require a lot of courage in an age when few people throughout the course of their entire lives ever ventured many miles from their homes. On arrival at their destination their welcome would be hostile as soon as their new neighbours discovered from where, and why they had come. Plenty of evidence exists of refugees from the plague being driven out with violence from their place of refuge. The people of Sheffield erected barriers and manned guard posts to prevent infected strangers from entering the town. Extreme measures were employed in Windsor during the reign of Elizabeth I where suspected refugees and traders from London were hanged on the gibbet upon arrival. Thus unable to travel far some of the villagers sought shelter outside the village, but close at hand and lived in makeshift homes upon Eyam Moor, or in the fields on the hillsides, or in the rocks and caves on the far side of Middleton Dale.

October saw 23 more victims including Jonathan Cooper, Mary Hadfield's elder son, another member of the Hawksworth family, four more of the Syddalls, five more Thorpes and several new families. The total number of deaths from plague up to the end of October (i.e. 29) now exceeded the average annual mortality rate over the previous decade. It was expected that the onset of winter would bring an end to their sufferings for they knew that plague was basically a summer disease, but the organism is very resilient for a relatively short period and would find within the cottages, warm conditions in which it could survive. Domestic rats would have nests in the thatch and rafters of the roofs and the wainscotting of the homes of the villagers, and comfortable rats would provide food for the fleas, who in turn would ensure the survival of the plague bacillus. In an age of poor hygiene there would certainly be rats in and around their homes. In addition to warmth, there would be no shortage of food. A look at the winter mortality does in fact show a big drop from the figure for October, but it was still well above a normal winter average. By the end of April 1666 there had been 73 deaths though this did include a small number who as might be expected had died from other causes.

Having survived the winter, there were natural fears that the summer would bring a significant increase in the death rate, but for some strange reason the total in May was only four, of which two were almost certainly not due to plague. False hopes must have been raised by this, for it would be known that things were getting back to normal in London, and in Eyam they must have had good reason for thinking that the worst was over.

Before they could be sure they were free from the infection they would look for a period of twenty one days without any report of a new case. Since the plague deaths in May, which were both within the same family, and both occurred on the second day, and the next death on the 11th is not recorded in the register as being a plague death, there were strong grounds for hope. Their hopes once raised however were to be short lived.

Chapter 4

The Time of Decision

Sadly for Eyam, the lull in May was only the end of the beginning. Though the total of plague deaths in that month was significantly lower than it had been at any time since the outbreak had begun and though there was much worse to come, there were many families who had already suffered terrible personal tragedies, among whom for instance were the Syddalls, where six members of a family of eight had been killed, and their neighbours, the Thorpes of whom all nine had died. In June, there was a sudden and dramatic increase.

Though most of the families would have found flight very difficult, some did leave, and certainly a number of children were sent away, including those of the rector, William Mompesson. Catherine, his wife, had begged him to take them all away to safety, but he refused, saying that his duty lay in the village. Later, he tried to persuade Catherine to take the children away, and though eventually they were sent to friends in Yorkshire, she stayed with her husband, a decision which cost her her life. Probably some time in June, when it was realised that the situation was getting worse, and with little prospect of any improvement in the summer months that lay ahead, Mompesson took some positive action. In the absence of the squire and the wealthier residents, who might have been expected to take control, the next obvious choice was the parson.

This would not have been easy for him for he was a new comer to Eyam, and something of a youngster in the eyes of the village, for he was only about 28 years old. He had only been presented with the living in 1664, having come from Scalby near Scarborough, with a young wife who was in a delicate state of health, (she was probably consumptive), and two small children. Strong winds can blow off the east coast of Yorkshire, but Catherine would have found little relief in the rigours of a Peak District winter.

There were however other problems facing Mompesson. The village had just emerged from a very troubled period. Two rectors, Shoreland Adams and Thomas Stanley had served the parish for 34 years. Adams had been appointed in 1630, but had been ejected by the Puritans in 1644 in favour of Thomas Stanley, who was himself removed in 1660, when Adams was re-appointed. For two years Stanley had remained in the village, probably serving as Adams' curate, or perhaps more likely as the Priest-in-Charge, for Adams held more than one living, and spent very little time in Eyam, preferring his parish near Rotherham. The two men were poles apart in their beliefs. Stanley was a staunch Puritan, whereas Adams represented everything that Stanley found repugnant and unacceptable in the Church of England. In the two years from 1660 to 1662 the situation must have been impossible and there could have been no spirit of religious calm. The parish was united in 1660 in its opposition to the return of Shoreland Adams and had in vain petitioned the patron of the living, George Savile, to reinstate Stanley whom they loved and admired. On St Bartholomew's Day in 1662, in common with nearly a thousand like-minded priests Stanley resigned his living. The Act of Uniformity in 1662 and the introduction of the new Book of Common Prayer in the same year made it impossible for him to remain.

Stanley returned to the scene, assuming he had ever been far away from it, in 1664, consequent upon the death of Shoreland Adams. He may have decided to come back to the village to be with his many friends after the recent death of his wife, who was buried in the village in June in that year. This was before the Induction of Mompesson took place in July. Little attention appears to have been paid in the village to those Acts of Parliament which were introduced at this time to prevent Dissenting Clergy from coming within five miles of their former parishes and re-awakening old differences and animosities. Before long everyone was far too busy to bother. Certainly the Earl of Devonshire who could have imposed the will of Parliament was sufficiently happy with the situation to take no action against Stanley. Thus he was able to spend the last five years of his life back in Eyam, and he died here in 1670, though you will search the churchyard in vain for his tomb.

There was a big difference in age between Mompesson and Stanley and almost certainly also in their religious views. Tradition has it that Stanley and Mompesson had little if anything in common in terms of their faith, and the influence of Stanley on this very divided congregation would have created enormous problems for the new incumbent. However as the difficulties created by the plague continued to mount they were able to set aside their personal conflict for the good of the village. The two men were seemingly working to the same plan and to an agreed policy, united to face the tragic events of the summer of 1666. Whilst today, it is Mompesson whose name comes more readily to mind, there are those who consider that Stanley was the real hero, and that he has been robbed of his rightful place in history. An attempt at the turn of the 19th century to re-establish him, resulted in nothing more than a memorial tablet in the churchyard.

It may have been circumstances that threw them together, but they probably ensured the success of their plan for the village, whichever of them conceived it, for in putting it forward conjointly they were able to ensure its acceptance from the adherents of each of the differing approaches to their faith. Working alone, either would almost certainly have failed because of the firmness of the differing standpoints of the villagers on religious grounds and the consequent rejection of any idea coming from the 'other side'. If there had been no other differences between them, people being what they are, many would look to the older trusted man that they had known much of their lives, rather than rely on a semi-stranger and a young one at that.

Whatever the details, it seems likely that the two men held several meetings probably in late May or early June, in the study in the rectory that they both knew so well and prepared a scheme, which they put to the villagers presumably at a public assembly. It is because of this historic meeting between the two men, which is the most important event that has ever occurred in the village, that Eyam has found a place in recorded history and draws large numbers of visitors to hear the story of courage and sacrifice, that took so many of the villagers to their deaths.

Even before they met, precautions must have been taken by others, and it was recorded by White Watson, a scholarly man who lived in Bakewell, who wrote as a very young man in May 1774, that the stream near Stockingcote had become known as Mondaybrook. During the plague period in Eyam, the people from there were not allowed to cross it to go into the Bakewell Market which then, as now, was held on Mondays, and so made their purchases through others from a distance, leaving their money in payment in the waters of the stream.

With the consent of the Eyam villagers three decisions were taken, each of which requires some explanation. The first was that from that point onwards there would be no more organised funerals and churchyard burials. The sexton, if he were still alive, could not cope with the demand for graves, and the clergy, with the assistance of Mrs Mompesson, felt that they were of greater service administering to the bereaved, comforting the dying and tending the sick, and with the preparation of wills, which was one of the principal concerns of Thomas Stanley. People were advised to bury their own dead, which they did in their gardens and orchards, or in the fields. Some of these lonely tombs can still be seen, though most have disappeared, and sadly some have gone in living memory. To say the least, this was particularly disturbing, for to their minds not to have been buried with their loved ones in consecrated ground, meant that on the Day of Judgement when all souls would be called to eternal life they would not be reunited with them in Paradise.

Many of these graves of course were unmarked, since the families were too poor to provide a headstone. In some cases the survivors would select a suitable small stone and place it at the head of their loved one's grave, having first gouged or scored a crude cross on its surface. Since most of the villagers were not literate the stones bore no inscription or name nor even the carving of the simplest initials. Though one or two such stones have been found, the graves themselves have long disappeared.

For fear of the corpses spreading infection, it was considered essential that they were disposed of quickly, and this was another reason for the lack of ceremony. Putrefaction was thought to set in very soon after death, the corpses yielding their poisonous infection to the atmosphere as soon as they were cold, and so they were dragged hurriedly to their resting place, probably by means of a sheet or blanket draped round the arm pits or perhaps simply a rope tied round the ankles. Some with slightly more reverence were borne on shutters or doors, and then tipped into their shallow graves.   In his *'Journal of the Plague Year'* Daniel Defoe tells us that the practice of burying the dead in graves six feet deep began at this time, the hope being that at such a depth there was no fear of infection rising from the tomb.   Stories have been told, though not about Eyam, of victims actually being buried before life had finally ebbed away, in the haste to avoid spreading the deadly miasma. Though several bodies were buried in groups, as for instance in the Miners' Arms' Croft and in Cucklett Delph, there is no official record of any mass graves or plague pits, which are a feature of many plague stricken areas, nor is there any reference to the use of lime, though there were lime kilns in the area. Anna Seward relates that numbers of bodies were buried on the hillside behind the church.

The second decision taken by the villagers, was even in today's terms, quite sound. They agreed that the church should be locked until the epidemic was over, and that services should be held in the open air. The precise details of how the disease was spread were vague and confusing, and in some cases contradictory. Some argued that it was a miasma, carried in the air, others that it was a contagion. There is more than one account of plague being spread by clothing, and people were very wary about buying new clothes at a time of plague. Samuel Pepys records his fear that his new wig may have been made of hair taken from a plague corpse.   One theory was that the disease was spread by animals, and Daniel Defoe tells us that the Lord Mayor of London ordered the slaughter of all the cats and the dogs in the town. He was so close to the truth, but yet so far away, for in getting rid of these domestic animals, he allowed the rats, the real cause of the trouble, to breed unhindered.

In contact with their neighbours, and certainly in dealing with strangers, it was considered that the minimum safe distance was about twelve feet, and here again they were moving along the right track. We now know that a plague carrier can spread the infection a distance of about two metres in front of him, merely by the exhalation of breath during speech, and that a sneeze, which was one of the many symptoms, was infectious over a distance of four metres if not checked by a handkerchief. It was logical therefore to reason that it was pointless to crowd together in church to unite in solemn prayer to stay the plague, since the very act of worship in a confined area would put them at much greater risk. The people, living as they did in a deeply religious age, firmly believed in the need for corporate worship and so consented to the services being held in the open air.

Some tiny streams run swiftly down the gritstone hillside on the north side of the village, cross the road at the Townhead and converge to form a narrow brook which has cut its way through the limestone, which outcrops at this point, and then suddenly bursts out into a natural amphitheatre, called Cucklett Delph, with high grassy slopes, on two sides, whilst the fourth, through which the stream escapes is now well wooded and so creates the impression of total enclosure. At the top of the hill on the far side is a huge outcrop of limestone pierced by the elements to form a shallow cave, somewhat resembling an archway or bridge. The Delph was thus an ideal place for worship, providing an appropriate setting, large enough for the people to congregate with the necessary safe distances between their family groups and yet holding them by its very shape in a united body. Mompesson chose the rock as his pulpit, and in the days when it was less wooded he would have been able to stand there and look across the valley, see and be seen and heard by them all, and so lead his congregation in worship and sustain their hopes. Anna Seward writes that to mark the centenary of the plague her father stood where his predecessor had stood to deliver a memorial sermon and that he could be clearly heard across the valley. Today an annual service of Thanksgiving is held near this rock on the last Sunday in August.

The third and greatest decision was to impose a 'cordon sanitaire' around the village in an attempt to prevent the spread of the disease beyond its boundaries.

Quarantine was then the only efficient means of controlling the extent of the outbreak, but it was hard to enforce and seldom effective in consequence. It needed only one or two victims to break it, in order to establish the infection elsewhere. If the disease had travelled to the nearby towns the results would have been appalling. It has been argued that the people of Eyam had little alternative; that most of them did not have the option of flight, and that their heroism was forced on them, but heroism is not necessarily premeditated, and as here, can be the result of the acceptance of circumstances. As long as the roads out of the village were open there was hope, but having given their word to stay, that hope, however remote, was gone and their awful end became inevitable. Such a decision could only be made by those with a firm religious faith.

Many will still ask why they did such a thing, and to that there seems only one answer. They were a Christian people with a deep conviction, and surely Mompesson and Stanley must have put it to them that as Jesus Christ had suffered death on the Cross to ensure the Redemption of the world for all time, so they were asked to offer their lives in a similar sacrifice if need be, to ensure the safety of people they did not know, in places they had never even heard of. "Greater love hath no man than this, that he lay down his life for his friends." For friends, read neighbours, and by the extension given in the story of the Good Samaritan, one's neighbour is he who needs help. It is a text they would all have understood.

Once made however, their decision created further problems. The village was not self-supporting, and needed food from outside. This was in no way unusual, but those who supplied them would only do so on their own terms. The price of food was their own immunity. To gain their acceptance of the plan to isolate themselves, Mompesson and Stanley had to assure the people that they would not starve to death. The Earl of Devonshire who lived in Chatsworth House a few miles away, was the chief benefactor, and arranged for food, and such medical supplies as he could obtain to be left at his own expense at the southern boundary of the village, from where they could be collected some time later, so that there was no risk to those who brought them. Requests for items that he could not be expected to anticipate, were left at the Boundary Stone, and were paid for as described below. The cynics may argue that his 'generosity' was a small price to pay for his own immunity, and they may well be right. It is ironic to think that in their hour of greatest tragedy the very poor people were fed better at the Earl's expense than at any time in their lives. There were at least two other 'dropping zones' on the hill above Eyam. Supplies, some of which came out from Fulwood, now a western suburb of Sheffield, were left at Mompesson's Well, as it is now called, which lies beside the top road to Grindleford, by way of the Sir William Hill, about a mile outside the village, and also at the more distant ancient stone circle at Wet Withens which lies on a now inaccessible part of Eyam Moor. The people of the village of Bubnell, which is adjacent to Baslow helped their stricken neighbours by providing bread, and old maps of that village show the site of the kneading trough and the bakehouse. Though there is no direct proof, it is highly likely that the nearer neighbours in Foolow and Stoney Middleton, many of whom had kindred in Eyam, would have shown equal concern and generosity.

It was customary for money which was left at the delivery point in payment of the goods to be placed if possible in running water, as at the well, and at Mondaybrook. This it was thought would wash "the seeds of the plague" as they termed them, from the coins, leaving them safe to handle. Where there was no water, as at the Eyam Boundary Stone, holes were drilled in the stone into which the money could be placed and then they were topped up with vinegar, which it was believed would have the same effect. There was nothing new or unusual about this plan. There is evidence of Penny Stones, Vinegar Stones and the like on many old maps, and Mompesson would be aware that a similar plan had been adopted about thirty years earlier, at Scalby, where he had held the living for two years before coming to Eyam.

There is no doubt that quarantine was effective in Eyam, and there were no deaths outside the parish. Stories are told of only two people who escaped and of one who foolishly tried to enter after their decision had been made. With our current knowledge of the plague and three hundred years of hindsight it is easy to see that if all the villagers had shut up their homes and camped on the hillside during those summer months, as indeed Andrew Merrill did, they would have left the disease behind with the rats, and the number of deaths would have been dramatically less.

Isolated from the world outside, the villagers waited quietly for their fate.

Chapter 5

Climax...

In June 1666 the death rate rose above the twenty mark for the first time since the previous October, but worse was in store as the weeks went by. In July there were 56 deaths, and in August, when the plague was at its height, the total rose to an awesome 78, which carried the grand total to over the 200 level. The death rate declined slightly in September as the summer passed its peak, to a total of 24, a figure we must remember that was equal to the average annual mortality total for the village in the pre-plague years. It fell further in October to 14. There is some confusion about the date of the burial of the last victim, which will be explained later. Mompesson, writing to his patron, Sir George Savile, at the end of the second week in November stated that, "None has died of the plague since the eleventh of October", whereas the parish register shows the last entry to be on November 1st.

For a long time it has been suggested that there were only 83 survivors, from which a pre-plague population of some 350 has been deduced. This is William Wood's conclusion, but as has been seen already, it was challenged at the time it was written, and has been queried several times since. Mompesson writes that 76 families which comprised about 350 people, were visited by the plague, but makes no reference to the number of survivors or of unaffected families. What seems to be a reliable indicator is the 1664 Eyam Hearth Tax return which records 59 taxed and 101 poorer untaxed households. The number of households, therefore is 160, and this makes Eyam the third largest community in the High Peak Hundred coming after Bakewell and Tideswell and points to a population around the 800 mark. By taking the names of the householders as given in the tax return, it has been possible, by using the parish registers to reconstruct their families, and then after removing the names of the victims, to trace at least part of the subsequent history of the survivors, of whom there appear to be around 430.

Further evidence is provided by a study of the post plague birth rate. It is known that women on average had a child every two years, so that those who had a child in 1668, with four exceptions were not the same as the ones who gave birth in 1667. Eyam was the largest element of a parish which comprised three villages, Eyam, Foolow (the smallest of the three) and Grindleford, (then divided by the river into two parishes). The number of women likely to bear children in the post plague years out of a surviving population in Eyam of only 83, was insufficient to produce 90 children born in the two years 1667/8.

An incomplete Hearth Tax return for the year 1670 shows 76 taxed households which again implies about 350 taxed people, but it does not list the untaxed households. Logically, one cannot expect there to have been any large scale influx of new residents into the village within four years of the end of the plague, and if all those who had fled eventually returned, their number when added to the 83 quoted by Wood, would have been nowhere near a figure of the order that the Hearth Tax implies, so there must have been far more survivors than Wood infers.

G.R. Batho writing in the '*Derbyshire Archaeological Journal*' (Volume LXXXIV) in 1964 at the time of the Eyam Plague Tercentenary suggests a population, some ten years after the plague of around 750. He bases his argument on the Compton Ecclesiastical return of 1676, which gave a figure of 532 communicant adults in the village, to which he adds a further 40% to allow for children under 16.

Leslie Bradley in his article, '*The Most Famous of English Plagues*' written some ten years later in '*The Plague Reconsidered*' reached a slightly different conclusion by taking 532 as 60% of the whole, and then adds the higher figure of 355 for children (being 40% of the total) and offers a figure of 887 which he relates to the whole parish as against Batho who relates his total to that of the township.

In 1881 the Rev. John Green, Rector of Eyam disputed Wood's population of only 350 in 1665 on the grounds that in his view during the ten years prior to the plague the annual mortality figure would be very similar to his own day. He could find no evidence for a wide discrepancy in the mortality rate per thousand of the population in the two periods. That is to say that 28 deaths in a population of just over a thousand in 1866 is roughly 25 per thousand and of 23 in 350 in 1664 is over 65 per thousand. There is other evidence which leads to the same conclusion. This view is confirmed by the Secretary of the 1881 Census Office, whose comments have been pasted into the Parish Register. They read as follows "from the statistical evidence produced, we think that the comparison of these averages is a good indication that the population of the Township of Eyam was not much less at the time of the plague than at present". The totals in the census returns from 1831 to 1881 average out at 1039 for the township and 1517 for the whole Parish. These totals may seem rather high for 1666 but they show clearly that the previous nineteenth century estimates of the size of the village were most inaccurate.

A detailed analysis of the registers does indeed show a much larger population and a greater number of survivors, and it may be nearer the truth to say that not 83 individuals, but 83 families survived. Whatever the likely total, it is however certain that the percentage of the population of the village that died was exceptionally high, and exceeded the 17% in London in 1665, or the 24% experienced there in the outbreak of 1563 (Paul Slack, *'The Impact of Plague on Tudor and Stuart England'*).

It says much for the honour and integrity of the village folk that having given their pledge to isolate themselves, they kept their word, and we know of only two people who left the village after that date. In such a tight knit community where everybody was known to everybody else, each death was more than a personal tragedy within the family concerned. It would be felt by the village as a whole; workmates, tradespeople, neighbours, friends, relatives, landlords and tenants; the links that bound them were many and strong. As they fell so quickly in the high summer, the stench of death that must have been in the air was overladen with a dreadful feeling of the inevitability of the loss that must surely come in one's own family; one's parents, one's children, one's wife or husband, oneself. What does become apparent as the current work to establish family relationships progresses is that the family tragedies were much greater than the parish register itself, and certainly the plaques over the doors of the plague houses would suggest. Whereas one might readily infer that two families with the same surname are related, married daughters having changed their surnames do not reveal their identity so readily.

The most poignant example of how families suffered is that of the Hawksworth family. Peter, his wife Jane and their child Humphrey were neighbours of the Hadfield's. Peter himself was the third victim as the plaque over the door shows. At this point Jane was in the early stages of a second pregnancy, and must have found life very difficult. It seems highly probable that she pressed her mother Sythe Torre to help out, who caught the infection in consequence. She died shortly after Peter. What is not revealed is that Humphrey who was eighteen months old was to die of the plague about 3 weeks after his father, but in that intervening period Jane lost her mother, her brother and his wife. Within two weeks of the death of Humphrey, Jane then lost her little nephew and her father. In the months that followed, other branches of the family, including those related by marriage were also stricken. In all she lost twenty-five members of her extended family. When the baby was born in March it was destined to die within a couple of days, but that is not recorded as a plague death, which does not make her tragedy any the less.

Similarly the Thorpe family, also neighbours of the Hadfields, suffered far more than the plaque over their door suggests. There were nine people living in that house all of whom died. William Thorpe left a will, but none of his kin living in the village survived to inherit and his legacies all passed to more distant relatives living in neighbouring villages.

As households were deserted and communal tasks were left unfinished, and as the cattle roamed untended round the street, there must have been as many prayers for their speedy release from their sufferings, as for deliverance. The news of each death would spread quickly, and the sight of the newly bereaved making their way to the rectory door to report their loss, or of the endless digging of new graves was seldom far from their eyes, and in August the account of the loss of a neighbour was scarcely finished before there was another similar tale to tell.

Suddenly, after 14 months, it was all over, and as Christmas of 1666 approached, though there was little rejoicing, life was slowly beginning to resume its normal pattern. Some of the refugees returned, children were heard and seen again playing in the neglected street, and social contacts were renewed, both by their immediate neighbours, and more guardedly by those in the nearby villages. In an effort to prevent a further outbreak in the following summer, there was "a great burning", or as one version of Mompesson's surviving letters has it, "a great burying", of everything that might possibly have held the plague "seeds". The rector set the pattern and destroyed almost everything but the clothes he stood in, as an example to others. Burning seems a much more likely course than burying.

Anna Seward, as noted previously, relates that a few objects were unearthed many years later, which she asserts led to a number of deaths, and there was a short lived scare, but the evidence is unreliable . Nothing else has ever come to light over the centuries. Since evidence exists from elsewhere that people were afraid to pass by plague graves, it is highly unlikely that they would have confidence in their future if they thought that contaminated objects were buried around them.

CHAPTER 6

...and Decline

What continues to defy real explanation is why plague which had been around not only in England, but also in the rest of Europe for over 300 years suddenly disappeared, certainly in epidemic proportions, in 1666. Eyam offers evidence of the last stages of its course. From that date there was no major outbreak in England. Indeed there were only a few relatively isolated cases, probably traceable to the return of foreign travellers. France was clear by 1700 apart from a disastrous epidemic in Marseilles in 1720, when some 40,000 people in the area died, after a ship, which came from the Levant, dodged the quarantine regulations and entered the harbour. The plague continued its retreat eastwards being more or less clear of Western Europe by the middle of the 18th century.

Many theories are advanced for this final disappearance of plague in Europe. The gradual improvement in the appalling conditions in which people were living and the use of new and more hygienic building materials played their part in the disappearance of the black rat and the eventual dominance of the brown rat. For example the use of slates and tiles as a roof covering in place of thatch, and the introduction of wall paints, washes and wallpapers instead of wood panelling and hanging tapestries and in the poorer homes more hygienic floor coverings, in place of straw, for instance, deprived domestic rats of much of their habitat within the house. All these are, however, evolutionary factors. The end, when it came, in England, around 1666-67, and in western Europe in the 18th century, was revolutionary and sudden and in the western world the disease remained of lesser concern compared with former days, until its reappearance in Hong Kong in 1894. The Hong Kong outbreak provided the first clues to its origin and course. Important discoveries were made, by Alexandre Yersin, a brilliant Swiss doctor, who had spent most of his life in Asia studying tropical diseases and to some extent by Shibasaburo Kitasato, a Japanese bacteriologist who had previously discovered the tetanus bacillus. In spite of these advances and the discovery of viable medicines shortly afterwards, millions of people still died in the Far East, then, and in the early years of the 20th century. The final break through came in during World War II, when inexpensive and highly effective medicines were developed. Thankfully pandemics are now a thing of the past; unless future wars are fought with biological weapons, which could release the disease again in all its fury.

Plague is still around today, though not in Europe, but such outbreaks are usually contained without fear of major epidemics, but there have been occasional fatal cases in the U.S.A. where plague first appeared in 1906. In Yellowstone and Yosemite National Parks there are warnings to tourists of the dangers of playing with the attractive wild rodents, whose fleas can spread the fatal disease. The World Health Organisation records annual small outbreaks in Africa.

More serious was the outbreak of plague in India in 1994, which was a severe testing time and made the western world aware of its dreaded potential. There was a serious and alarming outbreak in Surat, which quickly spread to Bombay 160 miles away. The natural reaction as it always had been was to seek safety in flight; not now on foot, or at best by animal transport, but in cars, buses, trains, ships and aircraft. Within a few days, cases of plague were reported in Calcutta a thousand miles away, and great concern was felt in the international airports around the world and particularly in Europe and the U.S.A. Dramatic precautions were taken and there was a massive and effective screening of passengers from the subcontinent. Equally importantly however it was possible to supply doses of the necessary antibiotics in their millions to the infected areas by the use of the returning aircraft.

Since then a very significant step forward has been made. Research, largely carried out in the United States and led initially by Dr. Stephen O'Brien, who is working in the field of genetics, has discovered a rare hereditary mutant gene which he has labelled Delta 32 that prevents the destruction of body cells by the plague bacilli. Because of the particular circumstances here, not the least of which was a relatively limited and static population, which has been carefully researched, experiments were carried out in Eyam in February 2002, which revealed that among the known descendants of plague survivors, who undertook D.N.A. tests, there was a higher incidence of this gene than had been found elsewhere. Perhaps of even greater significance in our modern world is that this same gene will also offer protection from AIDS. But that is another story.

Chapter 7

The Human Dimension

No account of the plague can be complete without reference to the many personal stories that have survived, which show how the people of Eyam lived and died in those fourteen months from September 1665. The oral tradition of the plague is rich in these tales which were collected by William Wood in the days before the bi-centenary and further researched and retold by Clarence Daniel, and around which have been woven a number of plays and novels which bring the people back to life in their pages. They cover the whole range of human emotion. There is fear, stark tragedy, pathos, affection and greed. Happily there is little of the cruelty with which some accounts of plague elsewhere are littered. There are even traces of humour, but they come more readily to our minds than to theirs.

Catherine Mompesson, the wife of the rector, having accepted her role beside her husband, is known to have worked tirelessly visiting the sick and dying until late in August 1666 when she too fell victim. Her ministry, in our eyes lies very much in the background, and this is highlighted in the Plague Memorial Window, in the north aisle of the Parish Church which depicts her as a shadowy figure moving behind Mompesson and Stanley. One of the symptoms of plague was a rather sickly sweet, cloying sensation in the nostrils, and one evening in August 1666 as she and her husband were returning to the rectory across the fields after hours of work among the villagers, she is said to have exclaimed, "How sweet the air smells," a sentence which filled Mompesson with alarm as he realised its dreadful import. She had never been strong and was unable to resist the disease, and so died a few days later.

He describes her death in moving letters which he wrote to his children, and later when writing to his patron, when he felt that his own death was imminent. She was buried by special arrangement in the churchyard, for this was some time after the decision to close it, near to the ancient cross which now stands on the south side of the church.

Her grave is now the only known plague grave in the churchyard, though nearby lies the headstone of Abel Rowland, which was placed there after it was discovered after serving as a flagstone on the floor of one of the cottages. This stone is of interest because it bears the date 15th January 1665, which seems to suggest an error on the part of the stonemason, but the man is guiltless because until close on 90 years after the plague the English calendar reckoned New Year's Day as Lady Day, the 25th of March and thus January came after December in any given year, confirming the date of Rowland's death as some four months after that of George Viccars.

There are mistakes on other tombs, and a careful observer will detect two on Catherine's grave, one of which must have been of particular embarrassment to him, for the mason got her name wrong, engraving MOMPESSEN or perhaps MOMPESSAN and a piece of stone bearing the changed letter had to be let in to it. A visitor to her grave on Plague Sunday, will find a wreath of red flowers upon it. By long established custom the wife of the incumbent of the day places them there because not only is the last Sunday in August close to the anniversary of the outbreak of plague in 1665, but also Catherine was buried on that August Sunday in 1666

Before the decision to seal off the village several families had left, including traditionally the Bradshaws, who never in fact returned, and the ruins of their once grand house are slowly crumbling. Bradshaw Hall was used as a farm, a store and a factory on its way to ruin, and is now totally neglected. The Sheldons who had property on the other side of the hill above Eyam took refuge there, taking with them their ducks, which we are told did not settle and returned to their home on the pond in Eyam. Andrew Merrill moved on to the hill overlooking the village and lived there in safety with his cockerel for company, until one day, having found the bird had deserted him, set off to find it, which he eventually did, perched on its accustomed roost, at the same time realising that the danger had passed and he too could return.

One woman who is said to have lived at the Townhead in the houses that stand back from the road, where the footpath is raised, being unable to bear the stress took herself off to nearby Tideswell on market day, hoping to enter the town unnoticed, to mingle with the crowd and to live in safety. A guard had been posted at the entrance to the town to prevent just such an occurrence, but the Eyam woman was a match for him. When she was challenged, she said she came from Orchard Bank, which is the name of the part of the village where she lived. The guard did not recognise the name, which is what she had intended, and when questioned further she was even more vague in her reply, quoting her Bible with the words, "In the Land of the Living." A disarming answer as he would think of Eyam as the land of the dying. The man's common sense was no better than his knowledge of local geography, for he let her enter, but she was recognised by other shoppers, and with the cry, "A woman from Eyam!", she was driven out, pelted all the while with whatever the terrified folk could lay their hands on. Tradition tells us that she returned to Eyam, a sadder but wiser woman, but her subsequent fate is not recorded.

At the eastern edge of the village a track rises up the hillside above the present road to Grindleford, which did not then exist. As the path levels out there were two dwellings, one belonging to the Talbot family and the other to the Hancocks. Richard Talbot was a blacksmith, well sited no doubt on the road which then led from Grindleford. These houses were the best part of a mile from the centre of the village and should have been far enough away to be safe, but somehow late in July the plague invaded the Talbot home, and all who were living there died.

Wood tells us in very romantic terms of the deaths of Bridget and Mary Talbot. "They were young and beautiful: they had sported with innocence and mirth on the flowery heath only a few days before death came and laid his cold, chilly hand on their lovely bosoms… and they had spent full many a day in chasing the many-hued butterfly amidst the busy hum of the wild and toilsome bees…". Touching descriptions indeed of two young girls, but perhaps a bit wide of the mark, considering that Bridget was thirty and Mary eighteen years old. Mary and Bridget were both buried on the 5th of July, to be followed on the 7th and the 17th by their sisters, Anne who was six and Jane eight, who may have been young enough to fit Wood's description. Six more of the family died before the end of July, and on the 15th of August 'old Mrs Bridget Talbot', widow of a former rector was the next victim. She left a short will in which she bequeathed her Bible to George Mompesson, the young five year old son of the rector. The last to die was Catharine, Bridget's great grandchild, a baby only 3 months old. One wonders who tended this baby in its last days. Does the answer lie in the next paragraph?

Since the Talbots and Hancocks lived away from the village with no other neighbours around, they would be thrown more closely together. Surely the children of the two families would play together, and this may have been the source of the Hancock infection or was it that, in an act of neighbourly compassion, one of the Hancocks buried the last of the Talbots, a task which would be beyond the capabilities of old Bridget, and which would cost them the lives of their own family. The first of them died on the 3rd August to be buried by Mrs Hancock in the field around her home. By the tenth, her husband and the six children were all dead and each day that week as the people of Stoney Middleton, in the valley far below, trudged to the boundary stone with their supplies of food, they saw her at her melancholy task.

This brings us back to the Talbot baby. Was it taken in and nursed by the Hancocks? Was Mrs Hancock's final act to bury the Talbot baby three weeks after the last of her own family? Was it this that broke her resolution and caused her to flee? Questions of course to which there can be no answers.

*The Riley Graves (the graves of the Hancock family)
beyond Riley Wood*

Catherine Mompesson's Tomb on Plague Sunday

The Boundary Stone

Mompesson's Well

But finally, broken and distraught, she fled from the village, and sought refuge with her one remaining son, who lived and worked in Sheffield and was probably an apprentice to a cutler. Through him the family name survived and prospered, and one of his descendants returned to the village and collected the scattered headstones of the children and grouped them round their father's grave. He arranged for them to be re-engraved, but they are again badly weathered, even though they are now protected by a surrounding wall and are in the care of the National Trust.

There was also one survivor in the Talbot family, George, the eldest son who, at the time, was living away from the village. He inherited both from his father and old Bridget. He eventually returned to the village and took over the smithy, and the family line survived in Eyam until the end of the nineteenth century.

One strange story in a slightly lighter vein is told of a man who entered the village. It seems that there was a shortage of timber, and the Earl of Devonshire made arrangements for one of his carters to deliver a load. If the wood was not for Eyam, then it was destined for somewhere in the Eyam direction, for the man was told to avoid the village and all risk of contact with the plague. Whether through laziness, compassion, indifference or sheer stupidity we do not know, but he must have entered the village, a fact which soon became known in his own village of Bubnell, some four miiles away near Baslow, and significantly only two from Chatsworth, which was the home of the Earl. The day was inclement and rain fell to such an extent that when he returned home he was wet through and developed a chill, the symptoms of which, sneezing, a high temperature and so forth are early symptoms of plague. Thus when his cold broke he was accused of having had contact with Eyam, and was isolated by his neighbours in his home and forbidden to leave lest he should in any way infect them.

The Earl ordered his physician to see the man, and advise him on his condition, less out of concern for the carter than for himself, for if the plague had moved four miles out of Eyam, it was time for the Earl to take his family away before it travelled the next two miles. There was a natural and understandable loathing on the part of the doctors to treat plague victims and they went to extraordinary lengths to protect themselves, and this man was no exception, but he dare not refuse. When he reached the house the poor carter was told to come out and to walk down the village street until he reached the bridge, which he was to cross and then continue to walk along the far bank. To examine the man clear of the rest of the village would seem to be a prudent course of action, but if the man expected the doctor to follow he was mistaken, for the oral tradition tells us that the doctor stayed on his own side of the river and conducted his investigation with some twenty metres of river between them.   It says much for the doctor that he was correct when he decided after such an unusual examination that the man did not have plague, and even more for his tact and diplomacy which enabled him to convince everybody else of the fact.

Few medicines were available, and none was reliable, but some sufferers did recover.   The chances were very slim, but it is perhaps not surprising that with a total of nearly 300 deaths we have a few stories of survivors.

The first and perhaps the strangest of these tales concerned Margaret Blackwell, who discovered her own cure.   Margaret's house still stands, though it is not distinguishable by any sign over the door. All her family had died quite early in 1666, except that is, for herself and one brother, though she had caught the disease and appeared to be in the last stages of suffering. So much so that on the day in question, her brother who had duties to attend to outside the home, was sure as he left the house that he would not see her alive on his return. Before leaving the house the man had his breakfast. He cooked himself some bacon, which no doubt would be home cured, and probably far more fatty than would be appreciated today. Certainty there was a lot of excess fat which he poured into a jug which he left in the kitchen. Shortly after his departure, Margaret, who was delirious and had blurred vision was overcome with a great thirst; all conditions encountered at this stage in the progress of the disease.   In spite of all her difficulties she left her bed and went in search of a drink, and finding the warm fat, which she took to be milk, drank it greedily.   This probably caused her to vomit, but whatever the immediate result, in the long term it was doubtless beneficial.   When her brother returned, not only was Margaret still alive, but she was clearly much stronger. She did in fact recover, and lived a full life, convinced that the bacon fat had cured her.

Some people were lucky enough to catch a relatively mild dose of the disease, and if they had a strong healthy constitution, had a chance of recovery.   But in this case, unlike that in many diseases, it does not confer a lasting immunity.   One such man was Marshal Howe, a lead miner who lived at the Townhead, at the corner of Tideswell Lane. Having recovered he saw a chance of turning his survival to good use, for in the summer months when the plague was at its height, there were families who through advanced age, or extreme youth or sickness had nobody who could dispose of their dead. Marshall Howe, believing that he would be immune, volunteered to perform the task for them, and established himself as the village gravedigger. When he heard of a stricken family he offered his services and having buried the corpse then returned to the house to claim the burial fee, taking whatever appealed to his fancy. In some instances there was no one left in the family to deny him, and in any case few would have dared to challenge him.

In later years he boasted of what he had taken in this way. Though spared himself, his own wife and son were among the victims in August. Some say that his heartless attitude was mollified by his own personal tragedy, but others asserted that it had only made him more ruthless than ever. One wonders if his work was the reason that his family perished. He may have brought the infection into the house after disposing of a neighbour's body, or by bringing home his 'fees'. It would have been easy for him to have been the means of transferring into his home a flea from the corpse he was burying, or in the items he had claimed for the burial fee.

To keep pace with his huge task, and ever mindful of the need to work as quickly as possible, some graves were probably prepared while the sufferer was still still alive, no doubt lying in his bed, listening to the sounds of the man at work, digging beneath the window.

It has been said that in Eyam there was no record of anyone being buried whilst still alive, but Marshall Howe came very close to it on one occasion. One of his neighbours at Townhead, a man called Unwin, was close to death. Marshall Howe had prepared the grave, and on hearing that Unwin was at last dead, proceeded to dispose of the body. This was often done by dragging it along by means of a sheet tied to the ankles or looped around the arm pits in order to minimise the contact with it. This is perhaps how Unwin's body was being moved, and it was doubtless the shock of it hitting the floor as it was dragged from the bed, or the bouncing it received as it went downstairs that stirred some spark of life in the unconscious form, for indeed Unwin was not dead, and he called out for a drink.

Marshall Howe was not familiar with the sophisticated state of an unconscious body, and thought he had heard a voice from the dead. He was not disposed to linger and fled, robbed of his prize, and more than a little shaken in his confidence. Since both men survived the plague one wonders at their feelings towards each other when they met on subsequent occasions.

The Syddall family lived in a cottage opposite those where the plague started, and as has been seen, were among the first victims. By the end of October 1665 John Syddall and four of his children were dead. He left a widow, a small child, and a daughter Emmott who was about twenty two years old and was betrothed to Rowland Torre who lived in Stoney Middleton, a mile or so away. During the dark months of the winter he made the dangerous journey each day to see her and be assured that all was well. Clearly the risk was very great, and eventually they decided that he would not come into the village, but that she would slip out and meet him, probably in the Delph, where he could be certain by her presence that she was well, and he would be without personal risk. Almost certainly this was done in defiance of parental advice, and all they would be able to do would be to look at each other from a distance and in silence, lest their plan should be discovered. Towards the end of April she failed to appear, and he feared the worst, but with ever decreasing hope he continued to go their meeting place. Eventually when he heard of the pledge the villagers had made to stay within the confines of the village boundary, his heart probably rose, his hopes rekindled.

When the plague was at last over and the village pronounced safe, he was among the first to enter, but a glance at her home soon told him the worst. It was empty and deserted, and he learned that Emmott had died at the end of April shortly after her last tryst.

For a long time the fate of her mother remained a mystery, but this problem has finally been resolved. The parish register reveals that Elizabeth Syddall, widow, married John Daniel, widower, on the 24th April, just five days before the death of Emmott was recorded. This was not the last act of the tragedy for Mrs Syddall, (now Mrs Daniel) for her second husband died in July, and she herself perished in the middle of October. She died intestate, but about the day of her death, she made provision for her son, in a verbal declaration to her friend and neighbour Rebecca Hawksworth, who immediately testified to that effect before the Rev. Stanley, and a Letter of Administration drawn up in the court in Chesterfield in April 1667 affirms that Josiah Syddall, the son of Elizabeth Daniel, who was only three years old was to be put into the care of her "trusted friend", Robert Thorpe, and that her estate was to be used for his careful upbringing until he was old enough to inherit and manage the residue. Robert and his wife Margaret had lost their own four surviving children (they had lost three before the outbreak of the plague) in the space of sixteen days in August. Clearly Joseph survived the plague because if it had been otherwise the Letter of Administration would not have been drawn up, but his subsequent life is not known to us, though the burial of a Joseph Syddall of Goldcliffe, a neighbouring hamlet was recorded on the 25th of January in 1730.

Great tragedy struck the Morten family, neighbours of the Kempes, who all lived well clear of the village beyond its western limits, though still within the parish boundary. Sadly their child had wandered off into the village in search of playmates, or as in the case of the Hancocks at the other end of the village had played with the neighbours' children, but certainly a similar pattern evolved. First the Kempes and then the Morten child were struck down. Mrs Morten was in the late stages of pregnancy, and when the time came, her husband Matthew set off to the village in search of the midwife, but knowing the state of things at the western end of the parish no one would venture to assist her. Morten performed the task himself, but with plague in the house it was not long before the mother and the new baby were affected and died, and Morten was left with only his animals for company.

That was not the end of the story however, for William Wood tells us that some time later Morten was walking his dog along the hillside when it ran off in the direction of a woman coming towards him, and made a fuss of her, thinking, as we are told romantically that it was his lost mistress returning. Tradition tells us she was the widow of Peter Hawksworth who was a near neighbour of the village tailor, and the third plague victim, but the register shows clearly that she was Sarah Furness, who at the age of 19 married, not Peter, but William Hawksworth on the 29th September 1665, six days after Peter's death. There can be no doubt about this because in the whole of the family history from 1630 to her death she was the only one of the Hawksworths to bear the name of Sarah. She was however a plague widow, for William had died in August 1666. She bore his child Elizabeth in March the following year. However there was romance at the end of the tale, for the parish register records that Sarah and Matthew Morten eventually married in October 1667, some six years before another tragedy in her life, for in 1673 her brother Ellis hanged himself in the next village. Sarah died in 1683 at the age of 37.

There were others who remarried after the plague, among whom were Marshall Howe who married a Mary Hadfield in 1672. This was not the Mary Hadfield, the tailor's wife, daughter of Thomas Mosley, formerly married to Edward Cooper in 1652, for Marshall Howe's wife was still having children in 1684, when Mary Cooper/Hadfield would have been at least 50 years old and in those days certainly too old to be having children. It is more probable that she was a cousin of Alexander Hadfield the tailor, who was 24 at the time of the plague, though even she at 42 would be rather old for having children.

Mary Cooper, otherwise Hadfield, eventually married for a third time. Her last husband was John Coe. The Eyam register does not record this marriage, nor has it been traced in those of neighbouring parishes, but Coe is mentioned as an Eyam householder in the 1670 Hearth Tax and his death, and that of his wife Mary are entered in the Eyam registers. However the marriage is confirmed in some Articles of Agreement drawn up in 1677, held in the archives at Eyam Hall, which relate to land bought by Edward Cooper and sold "by his widow Mary, now married to John Coe".

The last record takes us back to Mompesson. After the death of his wife he was distraught, and felt that his own death was near. He suffered from a painful leg infection during the time that his wife was alive, which she feared was a symptom of the plague but had treated successfully. Letters show that it was depression and perhaps exhaustion rather than disease which affected him. He managed to keep going and guided the village until the plague was over, during which time he wrote several letters probably as a means of recording the episode for posterity, rather than to provide information solely for those who received them.

Mompesson eventually remarried and in 1670, the year that Thomas Stanley died, took his new bride, Elizabeth Newby, the widow of Charles Newby, to a new living in the parish of Eakring which is near Newark, where he found even four years afterwards that his troubles were not over. Because he had come from a plague village he was not kindly received and legend tells us that for a long time he was denied access both to his church and his vicarage. This may be dramatic licence for both church and parsonage were in a poor state of repair, and Mompesson wrote letters appealing for financial assistance to effect repairs to the church which he considered to be unsafe. Among the archives at Chatsworth House are letters written by William Mompesson to Sir George Savile appealing for funds to restore the church roof before it fell and killed people. Mompesson's new wife was a relative of his patron, George Savile and owned a house in nearby Rufford Park which was the Savile Estate, which is almost certainly where they lived until the repairs were carried out. It seems far more probable that they would choose to live with a certain amount of style in a house of their own than in some crude shelter in Eakring particularly when there were so many difficulties about the state of the church.

Some distance outside Eakring is an ash tree rising from a small hillock, and it was here for some considerable time that he is said to have conducted divine service. Eventually he became a Prebendary Canon of Southwell, where he was a most active member of the Chapter, and later a Prebend of York, but he refused other honours, including that of the Deanery of Lincoln, which grateful people wished to offer him. He died in 1708.

The story ends in the strangest way in the following year where it began, back in Eyam.

Chapter 8

The Last Word

The Story of Eyam Plague really ends not with the death of William Mompesson in Eakring, but with that of Joseph Hunt back in Eyam in 1709. The Rev. Hunt had been appointed to the living of Eyam late in 1683 (and bearing in mind that the Gregorian Calendar had not then been introduced in England, this would be in March not December). Like Mompesson at the time of his appointment in Eyam, Hunt too, was a young man, but unlike Mompesson he was single.

Shortly after his induction he was asked to baptise a sick child, who was too ill to be brought to Church. The ceremony therefore took place in the "Miners' Arms" in Water Lane. Tradition relates that the child was the son of the landlord, a man called Fearns. However a scrutiny of the register shows only two baptisms occurred during the early months of 1684, neither of them being registered in the name of Fearns, nor indeed was this the maiden name of the child's mother. There was however a baptism of a sick child called Tristram Radcliffe, who died a few days later, a factor which suggests that this was the child concerned. There does not appear to be any family connection between the Fearns and the Radcliffes. It may simply be that they were neighbours, and the Radcliffes considered their cottage too humble and small, or maybe they had too many guests to get them all in! But that seems highly improbable. Those details escape us, but what is certain is that the Baptism Service was held in the inn.

After the ceremony the young parson is said to have behaved very foolishly and consumed more liquor than was good for him. It was noticed that he was paying more attention than was wise for one of his calling, to the landlord's daughter Anne, who was in her late teens. Eventually in the spirit of the occasion, somebody joined them hand in hand, and taking the rector's Prayer Book, read the Marriage Service over them. It is not hard to imagine the furore that would be created when the story was heard in the village. Even in our present relaxed age, such a scandal would raise more than a few eyebrows. In a deeply religious age, and in a village with a strong Puritan tradition, such a thing was unheard of. The Bishop of Lichfield, in whose diocese Eyam then lay, was less than pleased, and though he took no punitive action, he must have rebuked Hunt quite severely for taking one of the Sacraments so lightly. He did however insist that in the eyes of God the marriage contract was binding, and to make it lawful in the sight of men, he demanded that the service should be repeated with proper dignity in Church. The marriage duly took place on the 4th September 1684, and is recorded in the Parish Register, some six months after Hunt's induction as rector.

However, Hunt had previously proposed marriage to a lady who lived in Derby, and when she heard what had happened, she used her not inconsiderable fortune to sue him for Breach of Promise. The resulting lawsuit was very expensive, and the young parson and his wife found their resources drained, and their debts mounting. Eventually they got wind of the news that the bailiffs were on their way to the rectory to arrest them for failing to meet their debts, and they fled into church and claimed sanctuary, which at this date was still legal, but only in civil actions. Whilst they were in church they were free from fear of arrest, but their movements for the rest of their lives were very restricted. The bailiffs did not actually camp at the church gates, but if the couple had returned to the rectory it would only have been a matter of time before they were taken. In a previously published account of this episode Clarence Daniel says that the couple spent their whole married life from this point onwards living in the church, and that their two children, Mary and Sarah were born in the church. However according to the parish register they did in fact have nine children, of whom these two were the eldest, and so if the first fact is accepted, and it seems incontrovertible, then it must follow that all nine were born there.

Life must have been hard. There was then no vestry, and the heating and lighting would have been very poor. It is difficult to imagine how they did keep warm, for open fires were out of the question. In spite of their error, or perhaps because of it, Hunt and his wife were eventually accepted by the village and forgiven. Indeed they seem to have been quite popular, and at some point the villagers appear to have erected some sort of lean-to accommodation on the site of the present vestry, to provide them with some privacy.

Anne died in 1703, but her husband lived on until 1709. They were buried in the same vault inside the church, since the law at that time would have allowed the bailiffs to exhume the bodies from the churchyard and 'punish' them, either by casting them on unconsecrated ground, or in some more macabre way, because in life, they had not 'paid' for their crime to society. Their tombstone is now set in the north wall of the present vestry.

Because Hunt was unable to move freely about the village and perform many of the normal duties of his office, he took it upon himself to copy out into a bound register all the parish records, which were then written on individual parchment sheets, and so it is that all the entries for the period from

1630 to 1705 are in the same handwriting. It is quite probable that in his day the records extended back to an earlier date, for the binding of the book is loose and some pages may have been lost. There is certainly no title page which in itself suggests that it may have suffered some damage. In 1705 he handed the register over to his parish clerk. Was it in that year he finally came up to date and thus completed his task?

This unusual event explains why immediately above the entry on the page for September 7th 1665 there is a rather crudely drawn pointing hand alongside the words, "Here followeth ye Names, with ye Number, of ye Persons who died of ye Plague, imprimis." In no way could Mompesson have foreseen what lay ahead for the village. At the time of the plague, in the interests of the safety of the clerk, and also of the records themselves, or anyone else who might eventually handle them, Mompesson had dictated his record up on Eyam Moor, to the Rev. Walker, Vicar of Hathersage.

It is assumed that Hunt was working from Walker's contemporary record, but these originals have long disappeared, and one is grateful for this strange episode which has ensured the preservation of so much detail.

This explains why there are minor discrepancies between the register, and the account given by Mompesson in his letters written shortly after the plague was over, in which he states that 259 had died, and that the last death was on the 11th October, whereas, as we have seen already, Hunt shows 260, with the last burial on the 1st November, though the Bishops Transcript gives this as the 24th. Throughout the entire period from the death of Viccars to the 1st of November there were 276 deaths, and thus there are 16 entries in Hunt's list which are not numbered, and so recording deaths from other causes. This then accounts for the assumption that with just two numbered deaths out of the four listed in May 1666, two people in that month died from plague and two from other causes.

It has been assumed throughout that the entries in the register record the dates of burial, rather than the date of death, though when the plague was at its height these dates would surely have coincided since it was considered that immediate disposal of a body was necessary on health grounds. They may of course refer to the date on which the rector was notified of the death, or even the date on which it was actually recorded. Some delay here would have been inevitable because of the pressures of the moment, both on the part of the victim's kin and of the clergy, not excluding the vicar of Hathersage who was acting as scribe. This could establish the 11th October 1666, as Mompesson wrote in one of his letters, as the date of the death of the last victim, whereas the last recorded date in the register is the 1st November.

We must accept that Hunt was making a faithful record from the evidence available and neither omitted nor added entries, either as plague deaths or otherwise. There may be a clue to the discrepancy in the total in the fact that at the foot of the page for August 1666 Hunt wrote, "77 died in August", and then altered the units seven to an eight.

Many of the dates in October were omitted by Hunt, so possibly the original record may have been damaged, which could explain why it was not recorded. Hunt would obviously be ignorant of the letters that Mompesson had written and he would not be have been able to have a sight of the second copy of the registers, which still lies in Lichfield and which provide the missing dates. In making his record Hunt was unaware of how close he was. It is easy to be critical so long afterwards, but when one considers the difficulties under which Hunt was working, to say nothing of those which beset Mompesson, it is remarkable that such a complete record exists. One often sees greater confusion in statistics these days, when there are so many more devices to ensure accuracy.

The second copy of the register has been briefly referred to earlier as the Bishop's Transcripts. The clergy were required to maintain duplicates of their records which were handed to the Diocesan Visitor every three years when he made his triennial visit to Chesterfield and transferred to the Diocesan Registry in Lichfield, (now sharing the same premises as the Staffordshire County Archives Department) where it still resides. This transfer would have been made in 1668 by Mompesson himself.

There are minor variations in the two records, some probably due to errors made when the records were being copied, though no reference is made to still births and babies who died just after their birth. Otherwise there is great consistency.

Of great importance in the Transcripts is the discovery of a missing year in the register. When Hunt made his copy he found no entries for 1644 and 1663. The former, because Oliver Cromwell had ordered the destruction of the records and 1663, which had been faithfully kept and had been inadvertently handed over with the duplicate copy to the Bishop's representative in 1665 by Mompesson, a few months before the onset of the plague. This discovery has proved vital in establishing the truth behind the story of Mrs Syddall's small son mentioned in her will.

The story is told, the last word is given for the time being, but it is a story which remains fresh, about which new evidence is being unearthed, and which still excites the minds of both casual visitors and those scholars who are searching for clues to the answers to those questions that lie unanswered. The scene is like that of a huge jig saw puzzle with many pieces lost, some of which are occasionally found to complete another small section of the overall view. Perhaps further secrets are locked in unknown letters that lie waiting to be discovered, or perhaps there really is a cache of rotting relics, buried three hundred years ago that has escaped detection.

BIBLIOGRAPHY

A SELECTION OF WORKS OF NON-FICTION TREATING BUBONIC PLAGUE OR THE EYAM OUTBREAK

Batho	G. W.	Story of Eyam Plague	D. A. J. Vol. LXXXIV	1964
Bell	Walter George	The Great Plague of London	Bodley Head	1st Publ. 1924
Bradley	A. L. & others	The Plague Reconsidered	Local Populaion Studies	1977
Butler	Thomas	Plague & Other Yersinia Infections	Plenum Medical Book Co.	1983
Cantor	Norman F.	In the Wake of the Plague	Pocket Books	2001
Cartwright & Biddiss		Disease & History	Sutton	1972
Clifford	J.G. and F.. (editors)	Eyam Parish Registers 1630-1700	Derbyshire Record Society	1983
Cowie	Leonard W.	Plague & Fire	Wayland	1972
Creighton	Charles	A History of Epidemics in Britain	Cambridge	1869
Daniel	Clarence	Eyam, The Plague etc.	Country Bookstore Bakewell	1994
Hirst	Fabianl	The Conquest of Plague	Clarendon Press	1953
Honrox (translator)	Rosemary	The Black Death	Manchester University	1995
Karlen	Arno	Plague's Progress	Gollanz	1995
Kipte	Kenneth F	Plague, Pox & Pestilence	Weidenfield & Nicholson	199/
Marriott	Edward	The Plague Race	Picador	2002
McNeill	William H	Plagues & Peoples	in UK Blackwell	1976
Nohl Johannes	Clark C.. H. (trans)	The Black Death - A Chronicle of the Plague	Allken & Unwin	1926
Oldstone	M.B.A.	Virues, Plague & History	O.U.P.	1998
Peyps	Samuel	Diary - 1665 - 1666		
Porter	Stephen	The Great Plague	Sutton	1999
Porter	Roy	The Greatest Benefit to Mankind	Harper Collins	1997
Porter (editor)	Roy	Medicine	C.U.P	1996
Rawdiffe	Carole	Medicine & Society in Later Medieval England	Sutton	1995
Robinson (editor)	Brian	Seven Blunders of the Peak	Scarthin Books	1994
Scott & Duncan		Biology of Plagues	C.U.P	2001
Secrets of the Dead	Channel 4 T.V.	Riddle of the Plague Survivors (Recorded T.V.)	Tigress Productions (T.V.)	2001
Shrewsbury	J. F. D.	A History of Bubonic Plague in the British Isles	C.U.P	1970
Slack	Paul	The Impact of Plague in Tudor & Stuart England	Routledge & Kegan Paul	1985
Smith & Randall (editors)		Kill or Cure. Medical Remedies 16th & 17th Centuries	Staffordshire Records Office	1987
Tatbot	C.. H.	Medicine in Medieval England	Oldbourne Book Co.	1967
Turner	Derek	The Black Death	Longman	1978
Twigg	Graham	The Black Death. A Biological Reappraisal	Batsford	1984
Wilkins	Robert	The Fireside Book of Deadly Diseases	Robert Hale	1994
Wills	Christopher	Plagues	Harper Collins	1996
Wilson	F. P.	The Plague in Shakespeare's London	O.U.P.	1927
Wood	William	History & Antiquities of Eyam	Bell & Caldy	1865
Zeigler	Philip	The Black Death	Collins & others	1969

FICTION

Boccaccio	Giovanni	Decameron. Translated by J. M. Rigg	Everyman Paperback, etc	1st Publ. c. 1350
Brierley & Robinson		The Ring of Stones. T.V. film of rehearsal	P J Video	1999
Brooks	Geraldine	Year of Wonders. A novel	Fourth Estate	2001
Clark & Peggie		Eyam - A Rock Musical	Weinberger	1995
Defoe	Daniel	Journal of the Plague Year	Folio Society, etc	1st Edition 1722
Hoare	Edward	The Brave Men of Eyam. A novel	SPCK	pre 1909
Kempton	Linda	The Naming of William Rutherford. A novel	Heinemann	1992
Taylor	Don	The Roses of Eyam. A play	Heinemann	1976
Walsh	Jill Paton	A Parcel of Patterns. A novel	Kestrel	1983
Thorne	Monica	The Sweet Air. A play		1964